BIRDS and the TRICK of TIME

BIRDS and the TRICK of TIME

MARK ANTHONY BURKE

POEMS

CIRCLING RIVERS
RICHMOND, VIRGINIA

Copyright © 2025 Mark Anthony Burke

All rights reserved. No part of this book may be reproduced in any form, including electronic, without permission in writing from the author.

CIRCLING RIVERS
PO Box 8291
Richmond, VA 23226 USA

Visit CirclingRivers.com to subscribe to news of our authors and books, including book giveaways. We never share or sell our list.

ISBN: 978-1-939530-38-7
Library of Congress Control Number: 2025932885

Cover photo by Jean Huets

With love to Wanda, John, Kate, Colin, Jacqi,
Alec, Vanessa and Aaron.
Thank you for all your love and patience.

CONTENTS

DEDICATION | 5

I

LISTEN TO THE VOICES | 15
WHEN THE DAYS ARE SMALL | 16
PAYING ATTENTION | 17
INHERITANCE | 18
INVENTING GOD | 20
SAY THEIR NAMES | 21
PLUM SONG | 23
LET IT GO | 24
CAME AS RAVENS | 25
SAILING OPEN | 26
SOLACE | 27
TORN IN PIECES | 28
SEVENTEEN SONGS | 29
SNOWBIRDS | 31
SYCAMORE AVENUE | 32
STREAM | 34
LIVING ON THE LIGHT | 35
TOUCH LIKE THE WIND | 37
LEARNING TO DANCE | 38
THEY SAY THEY'VE SEEN | 40
UNDO THE FOLDS | 41
AROUND THE SUN | 42
WITHOUT THE LIGHT | 43
PRAIRIE LIGHTNING | 44
PAPER MAN | 46
IT RUSHES BACK | 47

PAINTING TALK | 48
HANDBOOK | 49

II

TIME TRAVEL AT THE PARK AND RIDE | 53
WHAT TO TELL THE KING | 54
LEARNING TO CONJURE | 55
RIDING THE PRAYERS | 56
ONLY YOUR EYES TO SPEAK | 57
WHAT I HID | 59
THE BLUE CHAIR | 60
SHOUTING ON SENECA STREET | 61
SOUND STARS | 62
TAKEN | 63
EVENING AUGURY OF THE WAXWINGS | 64
MATCHMAKER | 65
VOWS | 66
PICKING BLUEBERRIES | 67
WINTER PILGRIMS | 68

III

CUTTING CLEAN | 71
WHEN CATKINS BLOOM | 72
DOUBT | 74
LEARNING TO LISTEN | 75
HE KNEW SO MUCH | 77
DRY THE SKIN | 79
SMUGGLING | 80
TOLLS TO RIDE THE SPIN | 81
WHEN YOU WERE GONE | 82
PHANTOM LIMB | 83
MUSCLE MEMORY | 84
OUT OF LUCK | 85

CAIRN | 87
WHEN I READ THAT LUCIA DIED | 88
HOW THE COWBOYS LEARNED TO SWIM | 89
SOMETIMES THERE IS AN OPENING | 91
WHEN YOU WERE BORN | 92
SKIN OF THE DAYS | 94
SPOKEN BY THE SKY | 95
MOONLAND | 97
ROLLY | 98
BEFORE THE RUMOR SPREADS | 100
TRAVELERS | 101
SHE KNOWS | 102
THE NECESSITY OF LYING | 103
WALK AWAY THE GHOSTS | 104
VOICES CARRY | 105
WHAT I BELIEVE | 106

ACKNOWLEDGMENTS | 109
ABOUT MARK ANTHONY BURKE | 111

BIRDS and the TRICK of TIME

I

LISTEN TO THE VOICES

When breathing was still
a blessing given by the sky,
both lobes spoke in our heads,
one about when to follow the herds,
the other transmitted the gods' voices.
But when we began to chip figures in stone,
draw words on lambskin scrolls,
the two voices became one,
a single mind that invented sin.
This jealous god forbade the many
and dragged his cape
across his tracks to hide the slaughter.
Spirits banished to the forest and sky,
oracles began to riddle the future,
augurs interpreted the old gods' intentions
displayed in the flight of birds.
Only priests were allowed
to read these signs
and sold the counsel they gave.
I've learned that others among us
still hear the two voices,
follow and watch the sky.
Oh to be a soul who listens
to the sky-spirit chant in the wind,
who knows the language of birds,
listens when the lobes' webbing
opens and from behind our eyes
the old voices
spill their words.

WHEN THE DAYS ARE SMALL

November's meager daylight
seeps through the doorway
into the barn's dark shell.
The wind insists
whistling along the eaves.
The snow line has eased
down the mountainside,
advent of the frozen months.
The sheep file inside;
we stand together.
They inspect the corners.
The horse steps in
by degrees, cautious.
He presses his nose to my chest
and the sheep follow the old ewe
into the back stall,
come to hide from the wind.
There will be no other place
to find cover from the shriek
when the winter closes in,
the cocoon where I will come
for this company.

PAYING ATTENTION

You learn the timing,
who arrives first, who goes last
when the dark days close in
and October declares its rule of leaves.
The juncos search the ground;
you learn the order of things,
where you fit,
how each must devise a strategy.
In town, portents go unnoticed.
Made light masks the stars,
lures sparrows and chickadees,
into the trap of big-box stores.
Deft inventors, the birds are crucial
because the gods brought them first.
You become an augur,
observe an intent
displayed in the sky,
how blackbirds
rush apart like beads of water
blown across glass.
You see the courtesy of wrens,
sit outside at dusk listening
to the owl ask whose turn it is.
When a murmuration of starlings
pulses like a giant heart in the sky,
you divine a prophecy;
you will learn to sing without breaking
and that she will want you.
See how they morph across the open air,
how the swirling sheet
compresses into a spinning ball
and bursts into a thousand sparks.

INHERITANCE

A man survives by not giving up.
He sifts his doubt
through the mesh of the past,
finds what there is to save,
tries again.
I am a stalwart man.
She said she passed it on to me.
When she was small, she'd kneel
and pump the sharpening-wheel,
pedal it with her hands for her father,
blade edge riding the whirling stone
shooting stars into the shed's attic.
I've only seen him in a picture,
a wiry stern-faced man standing in a field.
He taught her a strict practice,
shear once along the ewe's belly,
keep the wool long for spinning.
In the evening, after the rosary's
government of pleas and admonitions,
he showed her how to card the bundles,
straighten, draw order from confusion.
Urine for mordant,
he boiled the wool in dun hues,
pots of burdock and beet-skin,
his hands stained ocher.
When he lost his words, gave up,
she strung her nights
on the loom's heddle,
learned the solace of patterns,
left to marry a soldier, passed on to me
the old man's taciturn ways.
It's always a search for patterns;
observe, connect, risk, persist.
The summer I quit school, a young woman
who'd walked the fields with me

sent a table loom by taxi to our house.
My mother had ridden
in a taxi twice in her life
and couldn't understand
sending it to me,
this way of giving.
I took it to a cabin on the island,
worked the days, a grunt's shift
on a lumber mill green chain.
Nights I'd try to build order,
rigged cross-thatched colors on the loom,
spent the days stacking wet-cut wood.
I ran words through the huge roaring saw,
spun sounds
until they webbed into strands
I hung on lines
in fall's low slanting sun
like dyed wool set to dry.

INVENTING GOD

Who spoke first to the sky,
conjured a name
for the lord of light?
Was she in the mountains
when clouds came so low
she heard voices,
dreamed she could walk
through the mist into the other world?
Was it when she knelt
in a cave of stone needles
and begged for her baby's breath
to stitch the light again?
Was it when a man lay
on his back in a meadow
floating a river of scents
and rose out of his skin
to drift the ocean of stars?
Or was it a day like today
when she walks down
the stone steps
with the last of her bags,
the little dog dancing beside her?

SAY THEIR NAMES

One already gone to the meat packers
the other to the bindery factory
before I was up for school,
we were all back by supper.
By dark, the three of us
left together again
to clean an office building.
My father divided the caverns of desks
between us, trash, toilets, floors,
the harmony of whining vacuums
droning through the castle.
Fifteen but I never said
how I had drifted from their god.
When the priest told them
there was nothing for me
at the Catholic school,
they let me leave.
I waited tables, hitch-hiked west,
worked on a sawmill green chain.
There were so many
sleeping in city-park woods,
each town like a cubicle,
the same square, worn place.
I walked for days, slept in libraries,
Greyhound stations, tried to stay dry,
tried to unravel something
without knowing what to call it.
They came from the island for work
and I tore them open
when I asked them to let me go
without knowing where,
a prince and a saint who
offered what they could.
I say their names every day,
gone to what they believed.

Even now, a comfort comes
from a vacuum's pitched moan
singing in the room beside mine.

PLUM SONG

In April, when the old promise
begins to murmur, bird song
flutters the air like confetti
and their notes fall
into the plum blossoms,
settle in their ovaries.
Each crucible nurtures a gift there
on a serum of water and light.
When the plums
were swollen with the sun,
a woman came to the orchard,
ate and sang the song
that had grown there.
I followed, wanting it all to last,
practiced an alchemy,
simmered the plums,
saved the voices in jars.
I found a jar, the label written
in her hand eight years ago
when she still sang
about the cruelty of lust,
the luck you have to spin.
Gone now to another dream,
the silence stuns.
You don't remember
how still the days will become;
a quiet forest,
a dead sparrow on the path,
the times you lift your head
to catch a raven's call,
hurt for the press of her body.

LET IT GO

When I came in from planting
alone in the mountains,
I saw your blue-wool hat hanging
above the boot bench
and the old tide surged.
It rains and rains here in the clouds,
taps your name all night on the roof.
I've made so many mistakes,
they pile up in the mornings
when I lie and count,
stitched to the bed.
I wait through wooden days
for the balm of your hands,
the times we stood together
in a line at the store
and you pressed yourself
against my back.
Tonight, when I heard the door
and felt you ease into bed,
I touched you but stayed quiet,
woke again in the dark,
got up to watch the blood moon
stain the sky,
let it take what I could've asked,
came back and gathered you to me.

CAME AS RAVENS

Cloaks black as widows
they strut the deck railing,
peer in the windows, leap away,
their stream of shadows
flowing across the ferns and rocks.
They peck at the doors,
smear saliva on the windows
that dries to a chalky cuneiform.
When I was small, she'd kneel beside me,
coach the story I couldn't believe.
But last night, kneeling on the kitchen floor
sweeping up pieces of glass,
dust rolled from under the stove
and her voice came into the air.

They glide from tree to tree,
compile their inventories,
drift over the swath of light
I cut in the crowds of hemlock,
a shrine I opened to the sun,
cast the ashes like seeds.
The winged mourners
scavenge offerings I lay on the boulders,
a lamb abandoned by her ewe,
stiffened hens tired of winter.
I sit on the porch and sift the past,
see her folded hands,
the raised tracks of skin,
burn scars from the bindery's vinyl-sealer,
listen to their guttural calls,
the clicked code they chant
high in the dead fir by the lake.

SAILING OPEN

Remember the night
we got stuck in the snow,
hiked a mile up
the mountain road in the dark,
huge flakes falling like ashes,
carried what we could
pushing through the drifts.
Mottled by moonlight,
I stand near the window
in the summer dark
floating the stillness as it falls
like snow on a windless night.
It's hard to know if it's true
that a conduit between us
conducts the voices.

Sometimes no messages come for days,
we walk on without knowing,
pulses sent but missed
spinning out into the sky.
It seems they arrive
not when you're listening
but sailing the air;
gliding on some reverie
a visitation
falls into your mind
like a leaf to the ground,
the words drift to you
when you stand in an open doorway
staring as the wind shows its face
in the long grass.

SOLACE

Up by dawn, pacing off a dream,
I walked down to the ocean
flooded with what I should've done.
In that early light,
two came from under the pier,
walked up the beach
through the morning fog,
a night curled against the cold.
Hiding under the forest of wharf pylons,
cocooned in the blanket,
they must've guessed at the tide's reach.
So many places are already taken
in the land of hide.
I saw them climb past
the closed arcades on the boardwalk
where the rising sun cleaved the world
into shade and light.
But I stayed in the calliope's shadow,
watched them stop by the pier railing,
choose a place, put down a hat
and begin to sing the way I wish.
Their third-above harmony
laced the air like woodsmoke,
slowed my breathing.
Light crept up the wall
lifting away the fog's shroud
and I rose on their melody,
the ocean's rush, the wind's trick
of taking ghosts
up into the sky.

TORN IN PIECES

We took in boarders when I was small,
men from the island who
left as beggars when the mines closed,
came a thousand miles for a chance
to breathe the city smoke.
Thrift-store beds in the basement,
clothes hung on a line
strung over the ringer-washer,
cardboard suitcases, little else.
I see them still
when I've walked away too soon,
how they held on,
pieced a life from so little.
Saturday nights at the kitchen table
they sang and played
penny-ante poker with my father.
Already sent to bed, I laid
at the back of the house,
listening to the rumble of their voices
hammer the dark.
Sundays before mass,
Francis would give me a nickel
to go out and pick up the torn cards
before anyone would see
where he threw them in the snow.
I dried the pieces, taped them together,
learned to mimic the voices.
Some are better at it,
flop a deuce and a nine
for a chance to draw another king,
choose when to forget,
pretend it's luck.

SEVENTEEN SONGS

Around dusk, I rode
the Bathurst streetcar to the stockyards,
walked past the kill pens,
gusts off Lake Ontario
braiding the cattle's lowing
with the boom of shunting boxcars.
A runner, I worked the night shift alone,
hauled skids of boxed meat
through a maze of cutting rooms,
warehouses and freight elevators
down to the loading docks,
buzz-saw of neon lights
shredding the silence.
I plowed the hallways with a skid loader,
sang out loud to keep the ghosts
from following me
when I passed
the windows of the dance-hall cooler,
the hanging bodies.
By midnight, I climbed
out on the sixth-floor fire escape,
looked for Orion, city streets
as still as a dead sparrow,
did the math again.
If I made enough I could
take the train across the prairies
before the snow came, start again,
find a band, scared enough now
to be a front man.
The day-shift men brought the light,
began again prodding each steer
up a walkway to the second-floor box pen.
Shot with a bolt gun,
the floor split open and the body dropped
down a chute to the kill floor, skinned,
gutted and cut into quarters

in twelve minutes.
End of shift, walking back
to the change lockers in the morning
I'd hear the shot again,
slam of the kill-floor gate;
the bellowed songs
of those who waited
silent for five seconds
until the laments started again.
Their voices stuck to me
like wood-smoke on my clothes
as I slumped at the back of the streetcar,
lulled asleep by the rail joints'
click-clack heartbeat.

SNOWBIRDS

I try to not lie to myself
in the early morning dark
floating the sea of what's gone.
First snow last night,
bird-feeder capped with an inch.
Gleaners search the ground,
scratch at the snow, towhees,
captives of our angled ellipse.
Wind shakes the snow from the trees
into sudden clouds
that collapse to the ground,
disappear in silence like the stars.
I go out, brush off their hanging house,
lift the roof, pour in the millet,
set a dish in the snow.
Chickadees and jays flit down
from the branches and fill me.
I remember how I wandered
the ocean towns along the Belgian coast,
lingered at dusk, waited until
the people were gone,
slept on the beaches, in parks,
watched the stars
flicker through the trees,
ancient news arriving.
I come back to bed,
inhale your sweet smell,
listen to you breathe,
begin the music
when you coo the sound of clouds,
the faint lightning of stars
through the branches.

SYCAMORE AVENUE

Gone away to find work
I stayed on the top floor of a fifties duplex,
walked the empty rooms,
climbed to the roof.
I'd look for omens in the sky,
watched the evening fall into darkness
near Pico and La Brea.
At night, I shaped life-size forms,
wire-mesh wolves, statues of women,
coated them in paper-mache, the room
crowded with goddess statues,
bodies standing upright, skin drying.
Thursday nights before garbage day,
I listened for the voices
I'd heard float up from the street
when the wind
spun their vowels with the rattle
of dead palm branches.
They scouted the walkways
between the apartments,
the boy lifted dumpster lids,
the girl picked from the sidewalk bins,
whistled if they found something.
The woman pushed a shopping cart,
carried what they took,
scavengers combing Sycamore Avenue.
I wanted to walk with them,
talk and move through the darkness.
Nights when the groan
of helicopter searchlights
scraped the alleys,
I'd wake and swim back through
a scatter of dreams,
gusts of a song about a river

blowing through the air,
go back to the front room,
talk to the bodies as they dried
leaning against each other.

STREAM

Dark matter is deduced
from how it pulls the light,
waves warped by some presence,
a sign of entropy's work.
There is a stream down
in the ravine behind the house.
I can't see it
but its melody plays,
drifts up the slope,
faint fumes of sound
rising like steam.
I hear the rumors of its rush,
endless chant of water
thumbed along
a kalimba of stones.
In the dark,
the traffic of living slowed,
its running washes the night
and I float away,
its faint mumble
stitching moments into the fugue
water has sung since stars came,
the dream that erupts,
muffled moan of longing
mouthed by its tongue.

LIVING ON THE LIGHT

The waxwings have begun to go south.
In the early morning dark, more jars
line his porch stairs, glass beacons
cooling in the half-light,
deep gold of peaches,
sugar baths floating pale pears.
There is solace in this alchemy,
the late summer practices,
saving what the light
tempts from the branches.
She left him years ago,
gone to patch the silence with voices.
He stayed to do what he's always done,
scalding the jars and lids,
saving what he's grown,
a cure for months of snow.
Jars line his shelves, reds,
deep navy of blackberries,
greens from pickled asparagus,
all in an order set by each ripening.
Miles up Nickelmine Road, his light
the only sign in the dark woods.
Nights in the kitchen by the fire,
he talks to the dogs,
the sweet scent of plums
braiding with wood-smoke rumors;
compote ladled into jars,
he steams out the moist air,
the weight of the world
pressing the lids tight for years.
In the morning chill,
after the jars of dill-brined
cucumbers are stacked,
he walks to the barn favoring his right knee,

labors up the loft stairs, talks to himself,
pushes a bale out for the sheep,
does what must be done.

TOUCH LIKE THE WIND

We spin away from the sun
until copper light glazes the air
and one mountain casts its shade
along the chest of another,
a mile-wide shadow
oozing down;
the tide of darkness
burying the forests there.
I want to touch you
like the slow waltz of dusk,
small gusts that stroke the air,
hands that rub the trees,
touch you the way
shadows slide
until a breeze
shudders the air
and you tremble
like the leaves.

LEARNING TO DANCE

Hooked on the two-four
sorcery of bass and drum,
I held up a wall
for half an hour at St. Jerome's
before I could ask the one
whose eyes turned ice to water.
I spun home through the night
between the streetlamp pools of light
lost in a trance for a year,
and woke when the plane
bumped down into Luxembourg.
The first days at the hostel,
I couldn't stop the fear,
took the train to Zurich, found
an old Tolkien jammed behind my seat
and carried him all the way to here,
hitch-hiked south and crossed
four days later near Chiasso
on a box truck into the Dolomites,
traded my boots for a sweater.
The new owner took me
to his family's stone house,
steep meadows, barn filled with sheep.
For a week I was a shepherd,
combed the high pastures,
followed the ewes, learned why
I had gone away.
Like a brother, he brought me
back to the road fork;
I didn't want to get out,
flatbeds and Fiats all the way to Venice.
Three days later I started again,
no rides past Solesino, evening falling,
I lay in the grass, read
until the light bled into darkness,

ate the crushed bread and cheese I'd carried,
slept in the field and in the morning
danced on the empty road
waiting for some kindness.

THEY SAY THEY'VE SEEN

The towhees that come to feed
just before night are gone;
wind has blown the clouds
past the mountains.
It will be a good night to try.
When the furnace begins
to grumble a call to vespers,
the rafters creak
and the steady moan begins.
I go to the window,
watch for the darkness to deepen
and allow the light-flow
of eons past to appear
streaking across the night sky.
It's then I go down to the water,
cast off and float the silence,
the sea of stars,
travel to a place far beyond
the grip of metaphor,
a time they say they've seen
in the fabric of old rages,
red hues shining a code
in beams of color,
a theology of light
announced in the firestorms of suns
that this child of ash
comes to watch.

UNDO THE FOLDS

Wind pulls back
the folds of night,
and a voice runs through my head.
It's better to let it land
like a bird that sees
it won't be caught.
A towhee swoops down for a treasure—
a tiny sarcophagus,
dried wasp in its shell of skin—
and I hear the words again.
Lambs come into the world
most often at night, slip through
from another darkness
in their gooey coat,
stand within seconds
to be lick-bathed.
In the early morning
opening the barn door,
I saw the small hind legs hanging out,
reached to tie on
a piece of baling twine,
seconds fumbling
to make this mercy work,
pulled it into the world,
heard the chant again.

AROUND THE SUN

We were born just before winter
when rumors of frost
stretch clouds into scarves,
Saturn bands that mask the light.
Moths circling a flame,
our first ride around the sun
came after the leaves had fallen,
those days they try
to tame the dark solstice
with lights and messiah songs.
I notice more now,
the manners of sparrows,
how they congregate on the railing,
how a sail of blackbirds
collapses on the telephone wires,
commuters at a train stop,
how the song of her voice
soothes me.
We've been so many times
around the light the bell
rings longer in the morning
but love is still the first wisdom.
The sky is torn with colors,
a frost glazes the grass
and they're hanging
the strings of colored beacons again.

WITHOUT THE LIGHT

The night the wind and snow
pulled down the lines,
we had to feel our way like moles
touching door jambs and
table edges, tentative
as new lovers.
We searched for matches,
some way to bring the world back.
Huddled by the woodstove,
we sat gold-faced,
cocooned in its glow,
talking as the flashlight dimmed
shrinking the room.
Opening cupboards and drawers,
we looked for candles
and you told me how you walked
your empty rooms on Sunday nights,
tried to find a way
to undo the loneliness.
I stared at the fire and I told you
how I left my wife for a shade
that faded within months
as we waited out the storm,
unraveling what once had shamed us,
the night making us brave
while the wind tore at the trees.

PRAIRIE LIGHTNING

After our tent was set,
we climbed for an hour to see
the sloped meadows above the tree line,
stared from a ledge across
the valley worn by the water,
river's carved ox-bow fingers
spread on the chest of the grasslands.
The land shimmered in the heat,
drafts swirling up,
flakes of the past settling below.
When the sky began to cloud,
I followed you down
threading the crowds of Ponderosa.
You started to talk
about your sister and your father,
how you learned to read his shadow
when he crept the hall to your bedroom,
how you could tell
from the way his hands slid the wall,
which room he would go to.
You turned quiet but when
we came near the edge of our meadow
you stepped ahead and started again,
told how you disappeared
when he came into your room,
learned to rise above your body,
hover like the saints in the pictures
your mother hung in the hallway.
We crossed the field in silence
to where the tent's blue peak
flagged above the seed-heads
and through the night with all its folds,
the steady din of rain
drumming the tent skin,
we laid inside on a bed of field-grass

listening to the wind rush the trees,
counted the seconds between
the flash and the thunder.

PAPER MAN

Your lie stretched for weeks
and tore one morning
on a contradiction.
In the last days,
I started to make a statue.
Evenings waiting for you,
I crimped sheets of wire-mesh
on a steel-cross armature,
made a six-foot man,
soaked newspaper in watered flour,
bandaged layers of glossy skin onto
the cross-thatched frame.
I talked as I made him,
opened windows to dry,
winter air blowing through.
I pasted on the paper, propped up
the hollow body with sticks,
clock hands scraping the hours.
When the legs stiffened,
I started again, coated the torso,
tried to keep him from collapsing.
You wouldn't talk, ignored
the stink of the soured-flour paste,
the person I was making.
I pressed pushpins into the ceiling,
strung threads to hold up the drooping arms,
braced the hands with stacked boxes,
wrapped the neck over and over
but the head still pulled down
looking at the floor.
By the tenth morning, hardened,
able to stand alone,
freed from the weight of any hope,
I filled a box of clothes,
left a note for you
with a name pinned to his chest.

IT RUSHES BACK

I found an auburn hair of yours
clinging to the couch pillow
and when I pulled it free,
a curtain opened on our story,
the time I carried you
through the flooded alleys near St. Mark's,
the day we rolled out of the mountains
onto your prairie
threading through on the asphalt stripe
across years of grass,
the tale we once built of our lives
when I offered you my meadow.
Does the downy woodpecker
still come to tap on your roof
the way he would
when the sun shone
through the skylight
and mottled us with shadows?
Say hello for me.

PAINTING TALK

It was what we could do together,
you and I, masking the edges,
working our way around the room,
covering every seam
between the ceiling and the walls
to make sure nothing
would leak under the molding.
I stood on the ladder to seal
the top edge, keep the wall color
from seeping through to the ceiling,
a line to separate the hues
and even after a year apart,
we talked only about the rain
and how to divide the tasks.
You took the brush to the edges,
defined the joints where one wall
met the other and I with the roller
covered the open spaces
as we spoke with our backs
to each other
turning the walls from tan
to a teal aquamarine, began to offer
stories of what had filled the months,
how it is to live alone
sorting the days into a life
as evening came
with the fading flat light
that makes you look again
at what you've done.

HANDBOOK

She gave her daughter a guide,
a handwritten book of wisdom
gathered across the plains of marriage.
There were pages on the slow
simmer of beef bones for stock,
how to draw out the flavor,
paragraphs on stain removal,
the temperature and time
to make preserves last,
how to bargain, how to save
something from each day for a time
when it would be needed more than ever.
But there were no passages
about how to rub his shoulders,
lean into his back at the store,
kindle the heat, graze against him
until he longed
for the salve of her weight.
There were no cautions,
about the huff and growl,
strange words in the dark,
no pages on how stunning
his need would be.
She learned alone how her touch
could fasten him, grown to her light,
about days of sullen silence,
what to do when the ache
pulled at her body
as if he was dying,
how the toll of time
sends a mind scavenging.

II

TIME TRAVEL AT THE PARK AND RIDE

In fives and pairs and singles,
a ragged parade of crows
drifts across the acre of white lines.
They go to congregate in a cedar roost
I've dreamed of finding,
two hundred murmuring souls
hushed into night.
From the bus bench I watch them
row across the last of the light,
slip off to where I've been
and would go again.
They say there is no time,
only a grid we're taught
to tally the waves of change.
Bent by distance and gravity,
there is never a common instant
to share with Alpha Centauri,
no moment there we could ever know
that happens at the same time as now.
A dam splits just behind my head,
a six-foot tsunami of moments
rushes across the park and ride,
lifts me flying
on the hot air of memory,
the cliffs along the coast at Vernazza,
the marble faces at Ephesus,
flower sellers in flatboats
along the Mekong.

WHAT TO TELL THE KING

Starlings spiral across the sky
until the speckled cloud
funnels down,
a spinning orb that
shatters into beads of water
racing across the sky.
In a breath
they draw together again,
flatten out into a flag
owned by the wind.
The augur would not prophecy
until he discerned a sign
to interpret for the king,
words falling into his mind
at night lying in the darkness,
the thoughts of the gods
revealed in the birds' silent ballet.
Crows banter and strut their mastery,
ravens chortle in the cedars,
announce a knowledge
hidden from us.
Standing on a ladder reaching
to cut suckers from the apple tree,
an epiphany arrives.
Revelation comes often
when there is no intention:
dancing in the kitchen
to a Kings of Leon song,
walking the evening woods,
it falls suddenly
from the air,
words appear in your mind
staring at the rain.

LEARNING TO CONJURE

Salt, yeast, water, flour,
your corded forearms worked
the ponderous shape into a life.
Standing on a chair to be
shoulder to shoulder with you,
you wove our days
from songs and admonitions.
Saturday, before vespers,
you flattened the last of the dough,
click and thump of the rolling pin
spinning on its dowel keeping time.
You ironed the dough into sheets,
let me spread the cinnamon sugar.
I bloomed in the sun of your praise.
Scrolls cut, rolled into bundles
and set to rise with the loaves,
we walked to church and I watched you
ease into the confessional
but I could not imagine
how you had sinned.
Years collapse, folded by time,
I try to teach songs and possibilities
to the young ones I've brought,
seed an open field
left by a faith abandoned.
Loaves out of the oven, sandman coming,
stove-light glistens on my votaries' faces.
They sing homemade ditties,
butter the bread people
baked with the loaves
and I drift on a kitchen voice,
the faint thump of a rolling-pin
spinning on its dowel.

RIDING THE PRAYERS

It was always a sunny day,
squealing voices flying the yards,
calls banging the air
but we would be inside
chanting prayers
along the circled chain of beads.
My sister somewhere in the sky,
we knelt and pressed our chests
against her orange couch,
said the rosary prayers.
I thought about how to speak
so that god would hear me,
if he could sort through
all the beseeching voices.
My mother ground the words
"blessed is the fruit of thy womb"
through the gears of her voice,
bowed for "thy will be done"
held in the onyx Our Father bead.
I tried to be good enough for two,
took a breath and climbed
each prayer's word-stairs,
caught my breath halfway at the top,
slid down the back slope
saying the words in see-saw cadence,
counted the tinsel threads
woven in the brocade fabric,
listened to the laughing voices outside,
how their words
mixed with the prayers
into funny songs.

ONLY YOUR EYES TO SPEAK

I should've listened more,
asked how it was
to nurse your father until he was gone,
what you wanted for yourself.
I wish I'd asked about
the time you fell against the table,
where my sister went,
the stain you could never get out,
asked about why you sent me
away to Catholic school,
the gowned crows, their sticks.
All the days alone, I left
for another darkness, the towns
and arms where I told stories,
came back with a box of questions.
But it had already begun.
You kept the trembling hidden,
buried the broken dishes in the yard,
tried to disguise your slur.
I hid from what was coming,
pretended it would pass
but each breath
became harder to climb.
Your head always nodding
to a beat I couldn't hear,
you walked off the tremors,
a twisted dance across the floor,
chewed at sounds, fought
to stay in the world of talk.
Near the last, after you'd given up
scribbling your notes,
we sat side by side on the couch
and you watched me
when I read you stories,

my listener from the beginning
telling me with your eyes
not to be scared.

WHAT I HID

I found one of my old letters
you saved in a basement box.
It was from a time
when I was living in a one-room cabin
up a mountain near Fulford.
I could see stars
between the wall planks,
cold enough inside
to freeze my bucket of water.
I'd written that I couldn't
get the dog for you,
trying to fix one day to the next.
After weeks I'd gotten the book
and the scarf you knitted,
started a job at a sawmill,
took the first week's pay in lumber,
patched the wall gaps,
tarred the seams to hold more heat.
You'd had your eye operation
and I asked if you could still read.
Books piled beside your canning jars,
skeins of wool in a box,
the timbre of your voice
seeped up into a cloud of years.
A sweater you'd made was folded there.
I smelled the wool for your scent,
wrapped it around me
as close as the day
you taught me to work the needles,
slip the loop over the point,
knit one, purl one, cast off.

THE BLUE CHAIR

Crayoned on the closet walls,
stickmen float like astronauts
abandoned to the endless night.
Browned grease coats
the kitchen ceiling;
slats from the shattered louver-doors
like bones on the bedroom floor.
It took three days to clean
what they left behind,
hangers strewn across the carpet,
a jigsaw mess of shirts, bedding, jackets,
detritus of giving up.
They left the legless blue-foam chair
their first child sat on most of every day
before she died last week at seventeen.
They learned what eye-flickers meant,
the syntax of gurgled cries,
head trembles.
Fed her spoon by spoon,
they slid her in the blue chair
across the living room,
parked her by the television,
went on with their lives.
They checked back in ten minutes,
looked as she stared
at the orange-streaked sunrise,
read her face for a sign,
saw her eyes
had stopped moving.

SHOUTING ON SENECA STREET

He strides the morning's rush,
screams a diatribe at someone
only he sees,
pushes his shopping-cart,
trove of bags and blankets,
up from the spill of tents
by the bridge abutment.
There is no vaccine for madness.
Days made of rectangles,
he paces his cage,
courthouse to the Paramount,
Westlake and back along the waterfront.
Where is the brother
who took him to school,
the woman who wiped his face?
He scours the alley beside the food bank,
armada of dumpsters, the cut-through
behind the food court,
scavenges for last night's leavings.
Shouted away, he swears back, goes on
plowing the sidewalk with his cart,
spitting a screed that infects
all the morning eyes.
Their faces harden to masks
and divide around him
as if he were contagious.
Three stories up, from a cubicle
I've earned by the window,
I hear him yell
both sides of an argument,
his voice slicing the din of traffic.
I sift his rant for a trail
into his world, watch him
lope down the street
as the rain begins.

SOUND STARS

Evening traffic slowed to a moan,
his coins hidden in the toilet tank,
he clips the tiny speaker-amp to his belt,
takes the white rod and steps down
saying the names of the saints
he's given to each stair.
His voice threads above
the parade of pickpockets,
jewelry carts and pimps,
his heart sailing when he sings.
It's better to live by the songs,
not just one in a train
led through the streets,
a hand on the next shoulder.
Night-women drop coins in his bucket,
men bump him off balance
but he's learned to turn aside.
They fear the dark more than he does.
The sisters taught him
to walk the paths alone,
click his tongue, listen for
faint echoes, sound stars
to chart his darkness.
He feels for scratches on the poles,
smell of fish stands,
bells on the massage-parlor doors,
tells time by the weight of coins
climbs the stairs again,
recites the names,
prays the days will be many
before he'll be made to walk
by the weight of another's hand.

TAKEN

Taloned gleaners glide the sky,
opportunists circling
high above the barn.
They drift down like leaves,
collapse beside what remains
of the ewe's body.
All matter transforms;
what was once part of a life,
becomes a piece of another,
a feather, a hand,
the rain that wakes me.
Tufts of wool roll across the dirt.
Flies on the ripped gut
rise in a cluster when
the thieves approach;
hooked beaks tearing at the belly
beginning the transformation.
They jump when I come close,
leap into the air, rise
and perch in the firs, watch.
The head is untouched,
eyes half-closed, mouth open
in a last stuttered bleat.
She must have been the last
to scatter when the cougar
broke from the darkness.
You never know when
the wand will pass over you,
see the shadow move
when it's too late.

EVENING AUGURY OF THE WAXWINGS

When the wind stills,
and the sky holds its breath,
the messengers gather.
Waxwings congregate on the willow tree,
light on the branches near the water
preparing to show what will come.
They dart out, flutter
in midair above the river,
stretch the moments until
you can see between the seconds
when the fire-service helicopters'
growling thrum whips the air
tracking the river's course
down through the canyon,
their tethered water-scoops
hanging like buckets above a well.
The waxwings mimic one copter's
stunned halt twenty miles up the canyon
where it swooped to drag the river,
fill its bucket in the whitened flow
until the roil of rushing water
pulled the ladened pail
and its ferryman
down into the deep current,
blades flaying the water,
stalled craft falling sideways,
as the motor wailed and sputtered
trying to restart, the windowed face
swallowed, flutter of the birds'
yellow-tipped tails
portraying his descent
into forty feet of silence.

MATCHMAKER

Where a choir on gossamer wings
once flew darning the air,
there is only quiet,
rows of apple and raspberry branches
lifting their blossoms to the sun
for the tiny visitors
who will not be coming.
A fume has spread among the callers
and turned them to paper husks,
bodies piled at the hive door
stilled to a silence
that stains the summer empty.
Through the week of blooms,
she goes down to the garden,
mimics the matchmakers,
walks the rows,
a conductor with her brush
stroking the stamens
directing a simple lust.
She tries to do
what the smallest so ably did,
stirs the dust of those
who must wait
to be asked to dance.

VOWS

When the days wore thin,
I came to accept I would go alone,
made peace with winter Sundays.
It was a station
where I stepped down
from a train of dancehall prowls
and would stay,
work the trails in the morning,
accept this as my abbey.
But a new moon called
and I stared across
a dancehall of strangers
at you standing by the door.
I joked, asked if I was in time,
and we began to tell stories
that took us through the night
and all the way to here.
My old people would've liked you,
how your girl's soul sweetens the days,
your voice charging the air like a song.
The camellia is blooming,
red orbs cast their halo of petals
and I see the chances that remain,
my beggar's heart tied to yours
for whatever the fates may bring.

PICKING BLUEBERRIES

Young men, before their lovers allow them,
before they learn a clumsy way,
should spend a day picking blueberries,
taking so that no stems are torn,
no leaves ripped,
the shrunken brown petals
from the first white flowers
falling to the ground,
learn by touch where to go,
to be careful moving their fingers
through the clusters of berries,
hold one separate from the rest
before picking, before pulling
those not yet ready,
learn how to judge the colors,
the readiness
when the skin's hue has deepened
and the sweet sheen appears
announcing one is ready,
learning to tell by touch
the willingness to let go.

WINTER PILGRIMS

How do the geese find their way,
only miles of jagged ridges,
the curved hip of a river
to mark their route?
I journey by song and word,
the sky's spill of flares,
moon's faint marble.
It took a day to drive to the cut-off,
climb the switch-back road,
swatches of snow between the ferns,
cold turning the rain
to a pudding of crystals.
Nights in the mountains,
fire-crack splits the dark.
I come for refuge,
hear no voices
that speak a written language,
counsel offered walking
the crowds of fir and cedar.
The trail along the hill's edge
ends where the clearing
opens its arms around the cabin.
Down the back slope,
through the curtain of falling snow,
they drift the lake,
keep away from the shore,
two snow geese and their gray daughter
riding an adagio of windless water,
gowned ships waiting out the night,
gone by first light.

III

CUTTING CLEAN

October grays with snow clouds
and what I didn't do,
haven't done; should've
split the rounds in spring,
cleared the ditches, graded out
the ruts in the road
before the rains,
should've answered her.
Seasons swell the trunks,
the wood grain warps
around broken branches,
knots blacken in time where sap
pools and bursts in the fire.
She'd say "in a gust, turn like a leaf"
but I couldn't hear,
couldn't see it was a gift.
It took half an hour before
I remembered to cut the bark first
on the birch rounds,
release the skin's grip
to let the wood split.
This stuck way hobbles me,
I miss the signs,
don't see the patterns,
how it should be done,
kindle the heat.
Balancing another round on the block,
I stare at the cut-face,
look for cracks.
I've been worrying for years,
bent around regret.
The snow will come soon.
I've lived this way too long.

WHEN CATKINS BLOOM

Blazing air warps the light above
the crematorium's chimney mouth,
wisps of smoke
disappearing into the sky.
I walk the snow-flattened grass
between the gravestones.
When I was small, I'd stand
behind him where he sat talking,
pressed my chest
against the ribs of his chair-back,
felt his voice tremble through my body,
followed him wherever he went.
But the picture of us leaning
together by the old Buick
never fit with the sting
of each slap's dull surprise.
I fell for years the day I missed
the railing when he pushed me.
Nowhere to stand
when he was in the room.
The nights he came home from work,
a blade in his voice,
I stayed in the basement
while my mother danced
to keep out of his way.
I left the urn buried under boxes,
his ashes souring
with what should've burned away.
It took eight more years before
the weight of all the nights and days
pressed the scenes into just one grief.
That spring, when the catkins bloomed,
hanging like jewels on the alders,
I settled with what was lost,
took the urn, climbed in the rain

down into the ravine,
carried it as he had carried me,
spilled him out
in the piles of old leaves.

DOUBT

The snow has fallen all day,
flakes drifting like leaves,
burying every scrap and hole.
Found one of the old hens
frozen in the hay chute,
brushed the snow off
the square boulder by the stream
and laid her there
offered to the sky,
the black scavengers that will take her
when I walk back up the hill.
I will show my children,
when they come to dinner today,
what carried me
over the hill of fifty
when I was tired with all my doubt:
this morning's twins,
two new apple faces
peering through the crowd of legs
in the corner of the ewes' stall.

LEARNING TO LISTEN

When my father passed in the spring,
I wanted to go so far it didn't matter,
left for Madrid with my middle one,
the guitar player
who didn't speak much to me then.
He busked off the square where we stayed.
In the evenings, I walked and watched the old people
take their little dogs out before dark.

When I was small, my father would call me "pal,"
a gift he spoke that I waited to hear.
I wanted to give this when my turn came
but after all the time apart, the silences,
I couldn't find a way to begin
that psalm with my own.

On the third day, we got to Seville late,
dropped our gear at the hostel
and walked until we found
the bar by the government housing
where they danced their solemn flamencos,
fan-strummed guitar, drummed cowhide chair,
a stone-throat singer tearing at the night
as carpenters danced with widows,
shop girls with old men,
each revealing their heart.

In the night, scouting for the street-names,
carved in the walls, he said what
the songs had done to him,
spoke the words of our old code
I'd lost out on the plains of fifty-one years.
We crossed over at Gibraltar four days later.
Searching the dark lanes of Tangiers,

gale-warning eyes scraped our faces
and I heard his "Got your back".

We slept that night by turns on benches
in the train station, boarded for Marrakech.
The train stopped three times
at the call to prayers and I spoke my own
holding what had come back to me.
We got to the medina as it darkened,
ate grilled lamb at the bulb-lit stalls
and I listened as he talked.

HE KNEW SO MUCH

I kept a picture, dried and brittle,
pressed between browned pages,
a talisman back to when
we'd just begun, when I knew
so little about how to undress her.
She showed me in the basement room,
brushed her eyelids along my lips,
stopped me from talking.
It was the winter before I quit school
and took the train out west forever.
Still at home with him,
I was drifting on songs,
two-four drug of bass and drum,
lost when all along he was there.
We didn't talk much,
he'd go to bed early,
leave for his meatpacker's job
before the stars were gone.
She'd drive to the house at night,
drag a stick along
the basement screen.
He must have seen her car,
must've heard but never said.
Nights came when I'd ease
out the downstairs door,
ride the empty subway
to St. Clair Avenue, trudge
the snow-banked streets to her apartment.
But what I remember most
are the Friday nights
he came home from work, showered,
poured three fingers of rye,
laid on the front-room floor
and listened to Mario Lanza records,
operas I didn't understand,

didn't think he could.
I want to ask what he heard,
if I could lie beside him on the floor,
hear him breathe, gone now
into the long stark winters.

DRY THE SKIN

His billowed song
floats up to my window,
opens the morning's wool curtain.
I lean out to watch him
jump over strewn scaffolding frames,
his awkward ballet,
the aria he sings stacking
bundles of ceramic roof-tiles
and slip back all the miles
to the last morning
we lay together
talking of the heart's territory,
its harsh topography.
I've begun to understand,
how the thread of days and nights
sews wounds into scars,
why you've taken your heart
to stay near the graves
beyond Missoula,
dry the memories
in the parch of summer,
lace them like a stretched elk hide
onto your rack of the past,
drum against what's done.

SMUGGLING

You made me promise
not to concoct another excuse,
not call again to hear
the soft leather of your voice,
stop taping poems to you
on the light poles of your street.
But the night blooms, takes me out
walking the path across the hills,
June nights on the river,
rage of water, boat of songs.
We took turns in the oar-rack seat,
ran the chutes, the pooled waltzes,
everything lashed to the raft,
only the voices of birds
beside ours.
Where the river calmed at a turn,
we tied off at dusk,
slept on the grass near the shore,
drank the stars, water's endless chant
sewing the dark.
Five nights, six days
got us to the take-out bridge.
Hushed by the presence of strangers,
we packed the car in silence,
too many after one.
I had to go back alone
when you visited with your sister;
lied that night
at the prairie-border crossing,
told the guard I wasn't
bringing anything into Canada.
But I'd hidden you inside me,
the wood-smoke scent of your hair,
your body and the dawn we lay together
peeking from the tent
at fox pups playing
in the wind-struck grass.

TOLLS TO RIDE THE SPIN

Like the shift in the bed
when you roll away from me,
I feel the earth lean.
One morning the wind
shouts and we spin away from the sun.
Cramped days of rain predict
the tolls to be taken for summer gains.
In the orchard, where I complained
to the pear trees after we argued,
an ice storm tears the branches;
the white flood begins.
Snow crushes the woodshed roof,
shattered posts like split bones
stab out of the drifts.
You go to town but I stay, keep the fires,
walk down the mountain to the mailbox,
find a card with three lines,
see how winter will be one long night.
At the pasture gate, I listen
across the silence for the mare's laugh,
hear her rattled wheeze.
Gone in two days, I claw a pit
from the pasture's sheet,
roll the body in with the tractor blade,
push a muck shroud over her.
I should have built a sleigh
before the snow got too deep,
worked a way down the mountain,
brought you back.
I may die alone if I don't learn
how to sift the day,
answer when you talk at night.
Two white craft
drift high above the pasture,
trumpeter swans crossing
before the mist turns to snow.

WHEN YOU WERE GONE

I washed your blouse and under-things,
hung them to dry outside
in the stone-rush of wind,
sleeves billowing as if
you were a priestess blessing
the gusts of sky and leaves.
I carried the cotton ghosts
inside before dark, piled them
onto your side of the bed,
a soft body I shaped
and spooned against,
the scent of you
still on the sheets.
I could hear
two breaths flow
like rivers into the bay of night
prayed to any god who would listen
and counted the splash of stars.

PHANTOM LIMB

In the early evening,
when crickets chant
to stitch the darkness,
I walked down to pick
the sour rubies,
knelt in the regiment
of five-foot raspberry canes
and looked for the sweet ones
not yet taken.
Down on my knees,
leaves hiding the sky,
I saw what I should've done,
the time that was left.
I looked for what the jays hadn't taken,
bent to reach the bottom branches
and heard a voice
calling from months ago
when we still braided our lives.
It sounded like you calling my name.
Dizzy from standing quickly,
I raced through a field of moments
looking to hear your blessing,
scanned the hill, waited.
But it was only
bed sheets on the line
slapping in the wind.

MUSCLE MEMORY

The body records its losses,
knots of memory
web into a harness,
an Inca tally cord held inside.
The instructor said to press backwards,
flatten our shoulder blades to the wall,
loosen, let the arms hang, release.
I closed my eyes, started drifting
down a river over brown-pepper,
gray and bone-white rocks.
A boulder there tore the rush,
lifted a glistening arc of water
up and over itself.
Trapped there in its eddy
for a five-second rush of dreams:
running through a cedar forest,
the same lucky ignorance
I'd gambled with through the days,
standing in a parking lot
holding a woman promising,
driving in his truck
coming back from the cemetery,
his smell oozing
from the plastic seat covers,
fumbled in the dark
for the door handle
and rolled up to the surface
sucking at the air in the room
wet with the past,
turned my face to the wall,
wiped it against the cold plaster,
held it there.

OUT OF LUCK

I hit the wall of body stink
before I saw them,
one in the open toilet stall
drying socks on the radiator,
the other washing in the chipped sink.
They rushed to pack up,
canvas bag, stitched backpack,
lives lived by the coins.
They'd have walked the night
wrapped in U-Haul blankets,
crouched from the wind in doorways,
lips drying to scars.
The Union shelter must've been full,
no more cots, no luck that someone
came too late, lost their chance
to claim a place at roll call,
mouth hymns for a baloney sandwich
and brown water.
They'd wait out the dark, warm themselves
by the Westin exhaust vents,
walk the downtown watching for police cars,
curl up by midnight
under the James Street overpass.
In the morning, after the food-bank line,
they'd go warm in the library; told to leave,
pan-handle at Third and Cherry,
tramp back to the shelter
an hour before roll call,
line up against the concrete wall
in the graying light, wait
to see if someone had faded away,
the five-second silence when a name,
called twice, floats away into the sky,
another gone, have a chance to spend
the night inside with sixty others,

lie down in the hot darkness,
their own eight by six rectangle,
one slot in the checkerboard grid
painted across the floor
in the old Bekin's warehouse.

CAIRN

When the old horn sounds
from two stars away,
I'll carry the stones
back up the mountain,
the ones I found when I climbed
fitting words into songs,
brought home treasures,
a whale's eye granite,
basalt frog, argillite shards.
I made a circle of them on the table;
at night it became a receiver,
pulled voices from the sky,
the promises, the pleading,
the short aching words.
When the days wore thin,
I'd go back up, search again,
stay through the moan of nights,
mornings when the crest ridges
tore the wind into songs,
came back down,
back to stringing words
into trances that soothed
my body like you.
When I learn the summons is coming,
I'll gather what will be needed,
climb through the light
listening for the music,
piled my stones into a mound
at the mouth of songs,
call all the names across the gorge,
listen for the echoes, lie down there
and wait for you.

WHEN I READ THAT LUCIA DIED

Streams rage with snow melt;
the waxwings have come back
darting over the water.
After the first clear days
I begin to cut firewood, hemlock
and alder pulled down by winter,
cut rounds to split and stack
in cord rows to dry,
shields of heat against the next siege.
Cedars sift the sunlight,
mottle me with shadows,
words fall out of the air
as if someone had just spoken.
It's not so much what you believe
but how you fill your days,
what you give.
When evening begins
to bleed into darkness;
I walk back
drifting on the songs of frogs
making their inquiries.
An old book about Krishna
says the soul is in the body
like cream is in the milk.
In the morning I'll climb to the clearing,
start again building the shrine
I carved in the woods for their ashes;
stab the pry bar
under another four-man boulder,
lever it to roll foot by foot
across the snow-flattened grass,
shape the circle wide
to hold the rain of voices,
light a fire for the living.

HOW THE COWBOYS LEARNED TO SWIM

We crossed the border at Kingston
in a '79 Ford crew cab
drove south dodging November snows,
all we had tarped-over in the truck box.
I wanted to start again, not be afraid.
We cleaned up at highway rest-stops,
cheese, jam and bread dinners,
kids sprawled asleep in the truck's cab.
Eight days and nights
got us all the way out to the Pacific.
I lied about a job, rented a Mar Vista bungalow,
backyard blessed with bougainvilleas.
The rickety carport was our fort,
good guys chasing the robbers
out to the badlands
where we rolled together in the warm grass.
I'd sit by our orange-tree oracle,
listen to balloon voices float the night,
coins glistening in the sky.
Up north I'd fallen
through the ice too many times,
couldn't find the bottom.
We got two sets of bunk-beds at the Goodwill,
a green couch and a kitchen table,
walked the evenings to Washington Boulevard,
picked through Ralph's "price reduced" bins.
Back with twenty-five cent treasures,
we laid on the floor in the front room
and I read to them about who made the wind,
how to swim in the ocean, the undertow.
Late at night I sifted the days for a hook
I could stretch into an anthem,
peddle to the percentage men
along the back wall at song-roulette nights.
Working phone sales, fired on Friday,

I'd start again someplace else by Tuesday,
a con on the tenth floor of a dump
near Sunset and Vine
cold-calling the east coast at dawn,
baiting plumbers, car-repair mechanics,
one sucker selling a score to another.
I'd get home in the dark,
calls in faint tin-cup voices
drifted from the bedroom
bargaining for one more story
to seal the night.
They were the keel that kept me straight.
Fired again in a week,
I hammered collections for a year,
hounded drowning men, anything to buy
the ground beef, rice and oranges,
keep the house, our private meadow,
strew of flickering constellations
where we learned to swim.

SOMETIMES THERE IS AN OPENING

In the half-dark, rain beats
a samba on the window ledge
and I slip off into the years,
that time after the dinner
as I closed the front door goodbye,
my father reached his fingers
through the door's small-barred window
and I held them for a moment.
Gone so long now,
I stand by the hallway picture
to be held in his gaze,
his "a little rain must fall."
Not past grade five, a child
sent to the coal mines, he learned to lie,
stole his way into eighteen and the War.
I have learned to lie too,
make up stories, dance with voices
to keep from falling
when the world spins too fast.
He taught me the rapture
of song and word,
the grammar of loving.
Let me scrape an opening
in the door between us,
call his name across the light,
push my fingers in, touch his,
press my lips against the grate
and whisper a song to him
I'm learning.

WHEN YOU WERE BORN

When your mother was carrying you
and the time was close,
I worked the night shift at American Motors.
On the paint line for eight hours,
I stood where the flow of metal shells
inched past on a wheeled conveyor,
scuffed out prime-coat faults
on the right-side of each body.
For fourteen seconds I'd sand
one side smooth as it dragged past
then read for twenty more
before the next body appeared.
I'd get through a page of Roman history
cover the book with a rag,
turn and sand, read, then rub again,
one after another after another.
One night I heard my name
slip through the din
in a voice like my father's
when I'd broken his rule again.
I knew he wasn't there
and read on about how Romans
made kitchen-spirit statues of clay,
thought how we'd dream out loud,
make ours glazed in blue oxide.
But the voice kept bellowing.
I saw the foreman marching down the line
and froze, caught again.
He shouted at me
to get to the hospital
and I realized you were coming.
I ran down the conveyor line
against the stream of metal hulks,
imagined your face and hands,

the table where we'd sit
working the pink-gray clay
into statues.

SKIN OF THE DAYS

Pull the sheet back over the hole,
lay stones along its edge,
stop the wind
from slapping it against the sky.
He showed me what I had to know,
how to brine the meat in salted water,
mix fresh dill with vinegar,
keep the cucumbers crisp
through the months of snow
when few would come the three miles
up the buried mountain road.
He taught me to talk to the mirror,
look in my own eyes.
It was a way to pierce the fear,
bleed your worry
when you saw it in your face.
He'd say make your own mind,
no one gets in the grave with you.
After we put him in
and filled the hole, a dent formed
when the mound settled,
caught the rain
and the grass grew late each year.
His steel on stone voice
still cuts the air when I cook
the oats and raisins;
even now I whisper the rules:
throw salt over your left shoulder,
watch a man's eyes when he talks
if you want to know
whether you can believe him.

SPOKEN BY THE SKY

By late September, birch leaves
trembling in the wind, we were late
to start the barn-loft's gambrel roof.
Weeks before, I climbed eighteen feet
onto the bare second-story loft floor,
flew above the cedars,
sang, laid and stared at the sky.
But the snow was coming.

Roof-truss template lines
drawn on the loft floor, rafter studs
cut and placed along the lines,
we braced together the first gambrel-truss frame.
One at each end as two propped up the middle,
we lifted the twelve-by-twenty frame,
slid the bottom studs out to the floor's edge.
My father's "it's a means to an end"
rushed through my head
and I wanted him to whisper to me
balanced there on the eighteen-foot plate edge.

Prop poles wedged under the peak,
two held the base to the edge board,
the other two pushed the peak up to the sky
fighting to still the wobbling frame,
hour-long seconds while one
rushed back to cleat-nail brace props
to the loft floor as I heard sky voices
come singing winter's curfew.

Pitched calls fell from the chevron,
stragglers pulling to catch the flock.
Scouts looked for water, a field
before the darkness came to confusion.
Iron smell of rain on the wind,

we covered the tools, climbed down,
made our way across the pasture,
first drops hitting our faces,
heading for the cabin's light,
one truss-frame pointing to the sky.

MOONLAND

He was so quiet when he drove me
to my hockey games, tires
squeaking down the hill
on the snow-banked road,
the city park's tower lights
shining on the oval ice rink below,
a grounded moon.
He helped me lace up my skates,
hands freezing, single words
making breath clouds.
But when I'd race up the ice,
his tenor cut the frozen air
with more words than
I'd hear from him all week.
Years gone now, his voice
slips from the corners
into the airport-hotel room
where I watch my son on a rollout,
some dream fright
shaking his body.
Come back from months of silence,
I want to talk with him
the way we wove our words
when he was small,
say how wrong I was
to lean away when he schemed
to hide the men.
Sixteen floors up, I watch
bodies inch along the sidewalk,
the planes screaming down to land.
When he wakes, we'll go out,
find a place to eat, walk
and name the morning birds.

ROLLY

Gunning second gear into a whine,
we crawled up the switchbacks
looking for the high pasture
held in the "palm between the slopes,"
come for his last year's hay,
the son of the son of the first one there.
Bent now but I could still hear
a song in his voice
when he walked us down to his fir-pole barn,
plank-braced trusses
sagging with the decades,
tin roof leaking light.
Sitting on a bale, he watched us,
work-swollen fingers laced in his lap,
offered a board to lay across the stack top,
spread out the load-strap pressure.
He talked about the winters,
snow piled to the windows,
summers, tomatoes big as never.
Years before he had a truck,
he took the horse wagon
down the mountain every Saturday;
wife gone now but she still speaks
from the window by the kitchen sink.
A crown of peaks
casts a three-mile shadow
creeping back down the mountainside,
avalanche of darkness,
pale three-quarter moon
floating up over the far crest.
Hairpin turns, careful not to ride
the brakes too long, I tried
to keep from leaning the bales,
drove close enough

to touch the inside rock-face,
moonlight glinting
off the streaks of white agate.

BEFORE THE RUMOR SPREADS

Up in the night feeding the fire,
the bone orb rises over the mountains;
moonlight spills patches of light,
shattered mirrors floating the lake.
His broken-glass voice
still scrapes the darkness,
spins me back to the morning
he asked where we go,
if what he'd learned
would be saved;
how to pack burl-wood in salt
and draw out the moisture
before you lathe it into a bowl,
how to keep going
when love seems to fade,
how to bank the fire so it lasts
through the long night,
how much dill for the brine,
how to carry the years
though the branches are bent,
how to watch the birds weave in the sky,
tell whether you should seed
on a May morning before the full moon,
how a body can carry such age
and hold a heart so young,
when to turn the other way,
let go, forgive,
how the peonies spread
the rumor of fall rains.

TRAVELERS

Rain through the night,
mosaics of red and yellow
strewn in crowds around their prophets.
Walking just after light,
high in the firs the black voices call;
squadrons of maple-seed propellers
spin down as the leaves drop
taking me back to my night,
the sister I dreamed of,
eyes to share the days,
mother gone to the light.
Pushing through the piles of leaves,
a hush falls after each step
and I remember how she said
you live longer
if you learn to let go.
It's a skill you must teach yourself,
a chant said out loud,
hold your hands up beside your face,
look in the mirror
and make the promise.
Twenty yards ahead
two white-tail does and a fawn
stand in the salal staring.
Their stillness slows the world.
They will pass the winter here,
days scraping the ground for shoots,
nights scanning shadows
the moon casts
across the snow.

SHE KNOWS

Each morning she finds him
packing the same bag
when nothing will be needed.
The man who once painted
crowds of dahlias
reaching for the sun
has forgotten their name.
He leans against her,
fingers of their cramped hands
braid into a cup.
She watches the wrens and chickadees
gather at the feeder, their habits,
how they perch on the vine-maples,
dart quick as a thought,
calls drifting like the echo of bells.
The flutter of their small bodies
has become her first comfort.
On the porch swing
she watches the light
lick the rocks as the days
turn from plums to frost.
She knows that soon
she will turn his body to ash.
They will go to sleep early tonight
and when she helps him undress,
he'll ask again about the bag.
She knows one day in early winter
she'll spread the gray powder
along their path,
hang his name on the air.

THE NECESSITY OF LYING

When they were small,
I'd line them up
before we'd go into a store,
spit on a tissue, wipe their faces,
straighten their hair, inspect.
They say now I was marking them.
I've watched how ravens raise theirs.
By fall, big enough to fly for an hour,
the parents lead the grown ones
away from the nest into the high forests.
They chortle and caw, follow to a new silence.
A book of myths and warnings
prescribes how fathers
should rub their newborns with salt.
The patriarchs dictated
that they must mark their children
to signify the covenant with god,
disinfect the corrupt tendencies
of the heart to ensure
their children would be truthful.
But it's no guarantee.
Though you believe they never will,
when they lie to you the first time,
you ache as though you've been cut,
and think you will never
close such a wound.
But you try again, reconstruct
the lesson of forgiveness.
You think for days
that it is a fault of your making.
But the lies are critical,
it is the way we learn to forgive,
the way we learn
that our eyes give us away.

WALK AWAY THE GHOSTS

A quick clap of wings
opens the morning,
swifts darting past the window.
Sunlight streaks across the trees,
shines through the gaps in the blinds
where bright bands
stripe you as you sleep.
You are as lovely as
the violet jewels of jacaranda
and still I am up and gone.
The old men tap
two fingers over their hearts,
nod a prayer of greeting
when they pass me
climbing the path to the temple.
They must know that I'm afraid
you will tire of my moody ways,
the hours of doubt and distance.
I have no medicine but to walk
and argue with the voices
until they melt into the light.
When I come back, please
come and we'll drink the red tea,
walk the gardens where the storks
have built their nests on poles,
watch the curved bone of moon
rise into the evening sky.

VOICES CARRY

Our ellipse determines
the steps of this liturgy,
rounds cut in spring,
dried in summer, stacked by fall,
burned through the months of snow.
The trees give so much,
borrow the light and water.
When leaves begin to fall
out of the mind of the sky,
I drive down to the stand of alder,
begin the season's sacrament,
gather the promise of heat
cut from the crowds after the thaw.
I heave a chunk onto the truck-bed,
loosen a memory, the time before
when you were here with me
building barricades against winter's siege.
More fits together now,
split quarter-rounds lock-stacked
in cord rows under the wall-less roof,
the hum of all-nighters
hovering in the roof's truss-frames
like a choir's last note,
what to take, what to give.
On another December evening,
when you come back
to build your own walls,
revenants of our voices
will drift down as the snow begins.
A solace holds
under the pole-barn roof
on a windless night,
huge flakes falling in curtains
past the roof-edge,
shrouding the last light,
the tamped silence.

WHAT I BELIEVE

After the heat of the day,
when evening had cooled the air,
I walked down to the pasture
watched the horses shake themselves,
stand and look at me.
They stepped out of the birches,
waited in their shy way,
drifted across the field
until we stood together.
Except for a breeze
threading the grass, changing its colors,
the pasture was still.
Out along the far side,
where cedars draped the split-rail fence,
a darkness turned in the shadows
just this side of the rails
then shifted itself again.
A fawn, late born, crept out
and stood staring across the open field
sifting the wind for a sign.
I eased around the horses
to better see this dappled spirit
breathe the dying day
but she burst her watching place,
leapt over the cedar rails,
became the dark again.

ACKNOWLEDGMENTS

Grateful acknowledgement is given to the following journals in which many of these poems, some in earlier versions, first appeared.

Adelaide Review | Learning to Dance, Inventing God
Adirondack Review | Prairie Lightning, Before the Rumor Spreads
Apalachee Review | Out of Luck, Sycamore Avenue
The Atlanta Review | Drying The Skin (Dry the Skin), Living on the Light, Phantom Limb
Avalon Literary Review | Learning to Conjure
Beloit Poetry Review | When the Days Are Small
Birmingham Arts Journal | Muscle Memory, What I Believe
Brushfire Literature & Arts Journal | Cairn
Burningwood Literary Journal | The Necessity of Lying, Seventeen Songs, The Blue Chair, Came as Ravens, Skin of the Days, Learning to Dance
Chariton Review | It Rushes Back
Chicago Quarterly | Matchmaker
Comstock Review | Still (Walk Away the Ghosts), Falling Through (Paper Man), When Lucia Died (When I Read that Lucia Died)
Common Ground | Cutting Clean
Dunes Review | Inheritance, He Knew So Much
Eclipse | The Two Lobes (Listen to the Voices)
Grey Sparrow Press | Handbook, Riding the Prayers
Hampden–Sydney Poetry Review | Ragged Chevron
Lost Coast | When You Were Gone
MacGuffin | Vows
Main Street Rag | Tolls to Ride the Spin, Paying Attention
Nimrod Review | Learning to Listen
New Ohio Review | How I've Wanted You
New Plains Review | When You Were Born, How Brave They Were (Say Their Names)
Nimrod Review | Learning to Listen
North American Review | Evening Augury

Poet Lore | Picking Blueberries
Potomac Review | Moonlands, Only Your Eyes (Only Your Eyes to Speak), Equitable Life (Moonland), Undo the Folds
Red Rock Review | She Knows
Roanoke Review | Around the Sun
Sisyphus Review | Let It Go
Southern Humanities Review | What I Hid From (What I Hid)
Southwest Review | When Catkins Bloom
Stoneboat Literary Journal | Sometimes There Is an Opening, Shouting on Seneca Street
Sugar House Review | Painting Talk, How the Cowboys Learned to Swim
Tahoma Review | Without The Light
Third Coast Review | Doubt
Tishman Review | Rolly

ABOUT MARK ANTHONY BURKE

Mark Anthony Burke's work is published in literary journals including *North American Review, Beloit Poetry Journal, Sugar House Review,* and *Nimrod International Journal.* He received his MFA from Pacific University in 2014.

Visit MarkAnthonyBurkeSongsAndPoems.com

www.ingramcontent.com/pod-product-compliance
Lightning Source LLC
Chambersburg PA
CBHW030529080526
44586CB00011B/374